snowflakes an d BOOGERS

AF430726

mark g. wright

illustration by
roberto custodio

Copyright 2024 by Mark G. Wright.

All rights reserved.

No portion of this book may be reproduced in any form without written permission from the publisher or author, except as permitted by U.S. copyright law.

A work dedicated to my son, Nolan Virl Wright.

I am trying my best to figure out the fathering thing day-by-day. I know I have made mistakes and will continue to make more mistakes – however, I promise you that I will continue to learn from them...and you must know that even if a mistake was made, I always have your best interest at heart (as difficult as that might be to understand sometimes). Being a father is the most rewarding thing I've ever done (to steal an adage from who knows when/where originally first coined).

The one thing that becomes more apparent to me each day is that we cannot take ourselves too seriously, and we must remember to work fun into every single moment possible (all the while learning) during this journey.

I love you, little man.

People Are Like Snowflakes

My mom and dad once told me that all snowflakes are different, meaning no two are alike.

They said people are like snowflakes too. No two people are exactly alike. People come in all shapes, sizes, and colors.

And just like snowflakes, all people are beautiful. That got me thinking. If people are like snowflakes, then boogers must be like snowflakes too!

Boogers come in different shapes, sizes, and colors. And since boogers are made by people—who are already like snowflakes—it makes sense!

Why Do People Do Such Silly Things with Their Boogers?

I like to watch people, even if they don't know I'm watching. It's a great way to learn things. Most of the time, people do things in the same way. But when it comes to boogers, people act differently. Everyone has their own way of dealing with boogers.

But why do people put their boogers in such weird places?

Boogers small, boogers big

Why must people always dig?

To find you up inside their nose...

And, put you places you should not go?..

Mom's Booger Blunder

One time, Mom was in a hurry. She was digging
through her purse in such a flurry!
But no tissue could she find, no matter how she tried.
So what did she do? She wiped her booger on her
pants behind!
Eww, Mom, that's just not right!

No, no, no, that's not right!
Boogers go in a tissue, neat and tight!

Dad's Car Caper

Dad and I were in the car, which he likes to keep
so neat,
But once he picked a booger and stuck it under
his seat!
Another time he picked one of mine,
And when he couldn't flick it, he tucked it in his
shirt's armpit line!
Gross, Dad! That's no place for a booger of mine!

No, no, no, that's not right!
Boogers go in a tissue, neat and tight!

Boogers small, boogers big

Why must people always dig?

To find you up inside their nose...

And, put you places you should not go?..

Grandpa's Soggy Surprise

Grandpa always blows his nose into an old rag.
And instead of the trash, it goes back in his bag!
He stuffs it right into his pocket with care,
With all those boogers still hiding in there!
Oh, Grandpa, that's not where it belongs!

No, no, no, that's not right!
Boogers go in a tissue, neat and tight!

Grandma's Secret Sneezes

Grandma thinks she's sly just because she's older,
But she doesn't know I'm peeking over her shoulder!
She picks her boogers and hides them away,
But I'll figure out where they go one day!
Grandma, you can't fool me!

No, no, no, that's not right!
Boogers go in a tissue, neat and tight!

Boogers small, boogers big

Why must people always dig?

To find you up inside their nose...

And, put you places you should not go?..

Aunt Mable's Table Trick

While munching lunch with Auntie Mable,
I saw her put a booger under the table!
She thought no one was looking, but I did see,
Aunt Mable, don't you know boogers spread
germs like a sneeze?

No, no, no, that's not right!
Boogers go in a tissue, neat and tight!

Uncle Jimmy's Flicking Fun

Uncle Jimmy loves to flick his boogers for fun,
He once flicked one at his sister, and boy,
did she run!
With a quick little flick of his knuckles so quick,
He made sure his booger would really stick!
Oh, Uncle Jimmy, that's so gross!

No, no, no, that's not right!
Boogers go in a tissue, neat and tight!

Boogers small, boogers big

Why must people always dig?

To find you up inside their nose...

And, put you places you should not go?..

Teacher's Book Booger

I once saw my teacher, Miss Sue,
Pick a booger right out of her nose – it's true!
She placed it inside a big blue book,
Way up on the shelf, hidden in the nook.
Miss Sue, I hope you don't forget where it is!

No, no, no, that's not right!
Boogers go in a tissue, neat and tight!

Jamie's Tasty Treat

My friend Jamie is the funniest guy,
He eats his boogers and I don't know why!
He calls them snacks, like they're a treat,
He says they're salty, not too sweet!
Jamie, I'll stick with my sandwiches, thank you!

No, no, no, that's not right!
Boogers go in a tissue, neat and tight!

Jake the Friendly Dog

Even my dog Jake isn't booger-free,
When he has a runny nose, he runs straight to me!
He rubs his nose on my pants or my shirt,
And sometimes even on my friend's favorite skirt!
But everyone thinks Jake's just being friendly!

No, no, no, that's not right!
Boogers go in a tissue, neat and tight!

The Booger Sculptor in the Park

There's this guy who sleeps on a bench in the park,
Where Mom and Dad take me before it gets dark.
He's made a sculpture with boogers so green,
The weirdest thing I've ever seen!
I wonder if he knows that's a little bit strange?

No, no, no, that's not right!
Boogers go in a tissue, neat and tight!

Boogers small, boogers big

Why must people always dig?

To find you up inside their nose...

And, put you places you should not go?..

The Clean Snowflake

I think everyone is so silly and gross.
The only place boogers should go is in a tissue,
of course!
(Why would they not?)
If people really are like snowflakes, I'd like to be
a clean, pretty, fresh snowflake,
Not like one of those booger snowflakes!

So remember, kids, next time you feel a
sneeze or a pick,
Grab a tissue quick—make it your handy trick!
Let's all be snowflakes, fresh and clean,
And keep our noses germ-free and NOT green!

The End

www.ingramcontent.com/pod-product-compliance
Lightning Source LLC
Chambersburg PA
CBHW042136110726
48006CB00003B/895